PREVENTING BURNOUT

The key to staying healthy
and engaged at work

Written by Priscillia Mommens-Valenduc
Translated by Rebecca Neal

Coaching 50MINUTES.com

BURNOUT

- **Issue:** how can I avoid getting trapped in the vicious circle of burnout?
- **Uses:** this guide will help you to put things in perspective and manage your emotions better, know and stick to your limits, and be kinder to yourself and slow down.
- **Professional context:** health and wellbeing at work.
- **FAQs:**
  - How can burnout be recognised?
  - Stress or burnout: when should you worry?
  - Are there any high-risk professions?
  - Is burnout an illness?
  - Is burnout recognised by the law?
  - Is burnout contagious?
  - Who should you talk to if you are experiencing burnout?

Work is more than just your way of making a living: it's your passion! Every day, you throw everything you have into accomplishing your tasks, delivering quality and reaching, or even surpassing, your goals. You are conscientious, a perfectionist even, and you aim for recognition at all costs. With this in mind, you never object to taking on work and don't think twice about working overtime. The first to arrive and the last to leave, you tend to take work home "just to finish off". You push yourself to the limit and are brimming with motivation and energy. You always do more, but could you be doing too much?

Over time, your relaxation time gets shorter and evenings with family and friends become rare. Your mind is constantly on work, leaving no space for your private life. And deep down inside you, there is a ball of stress that never goes away. Your tired, worn-out body can no longer keep up with this hellish pace. Faced with overload, you are no longer up to the challenge: you make a string of mistakes, you have lost your taste for work and a feeling of failure overwhelms you, to the point that you lose all your self-esteem. The process began without warning, and you never saw it coming. You realise now but it is too late: burnout has taken hold of you.

How can you avoid getting to this point of no return? Learn to protect yourself, listen to your body and strike a balance. Spot the warning signs of burnout and identify risky behaviours before you lose control for good.

BURNOUT: THE BASICS

WHAT IS BURNOUT?

For more than a decade now, the media has been warning us about this scourge of modern times: burnout. The verb "to burn out" literally means "to become or cause to become worn out or inoperative" (*Collins English Dictionary*). As such, a person who is burnt out is so exhausted by their work that they can no longer function. They feel intense physical and psychological fatigue, resulting from a feeling of powerlessness and despair.

Burnout in literature

The concept of burnout is inspired by the aerospace industry. Originally, the term described a rocket which was running low on fuel and whose engine had overheated, putting it at risk of explosion.

The word burnout was first used in an article to designate a psychological phenomenon specific to the world of work in 1969. The author, Harold Bradley, recommended putting in place a structure designed to protect probation officers working in a community-based treatment programme for juvenile delinquents from burnout.

In 1974, burnout was the subject of a new article written by Herbert Freudenberger. Freudenberger, who was a psychologist in a drug addiction clinic in New York, described the process of demoralisation, disillusionment and exhaustion that he noted in volunteers. The psychoanalyst and doctor had himself suffered from burnout on two occasions, and this no doubt contributed to the credibility of his writing on the subject. Today, he is considered to be the spiritual father of the concept. Through the metaphorical image of an "inner burning", Freudenberger compares individuals to buildings which have been struck by fire:

> "What had once been a throbbing, vital structure is now deserted. Where there had once been activity, there are now only crumbling reminders of energy and life. Some bricks or concrete may be left; some outline of windows. Indeed, the outer shell may seem almost intact. Only if you venture inside will you be struck by the full force of the desolation." (Freudenberger and Richelson, 1980)

In 1976, as part of her research in social psychology, Christina Maslach expanded the concept of burnout, which until then had been limited to mental health professionals, to cover all individuals whose jobs require a high level of emotional and social commitment. This group includes not only medical staff, but also social workers, teachers and lawyers.

Burnout today

Since it was first accepted, the definition of burnout has constantly been fine-tuned. Although many doctors and authors have addressed the issue, they all agree on one point: the source of the process can be found in the professional environment. While it was thought in the 1960s that burnout was limited to the "helping" professions, since the end of the 1980s analysts and doctors have agreed that the syndrome affects a much larger proportion of workers: it is a genuine social phenomenon and no sector of activity is completely free from it. Research is still being carried out on the problem's potential contributing factors and treatment.

THE THREE DIMENSIONS OF BURNOUT

The studies carried out by Christina Maslach made a major contribution to the definition of the main characteristics of burnout and its diagnosis at the end of the 1970s. In 1981, alongside the psychiatrist Susan Jackson, Maslach dedicated herself to developing a method which would allow the syndrome to be measured. To do this, Maslach and Jackson identified the three main dimensions of burnout: emotional exhaustion, depersonalisation and reduced personal accomplishment.

The three dimensions of burnout

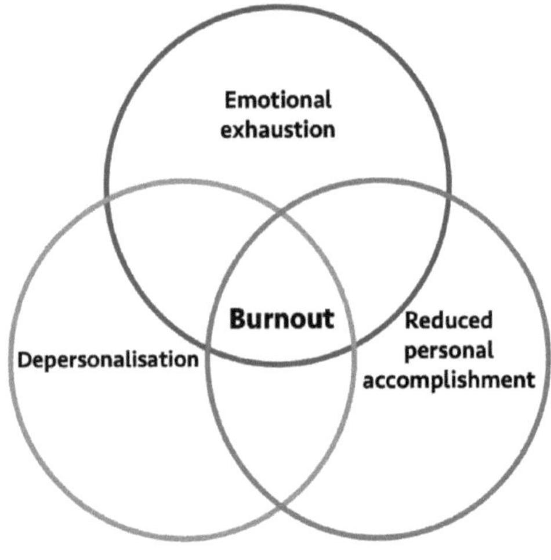

Emotional exhaustion

A person suffering from burnout feels psychological and physiological pressure at all times. Facing the stress, anxiety, intense fatigue and/or insomnia that now form the pattern of their everyday life, the individual feels literally drained of their emotional resources.

Depersonalisation

Completely exhausted, the person decides to "harden themselves" to the world around them, protecting themselves from any affective load through depersonalisation. They come to consider others as objects or numbers rather than as human beings in their own right. In this way, they develop a lack of sensitivity, as well as a negative view of other people and of work in general. Depersonalisation (also known as "cynicism") functions in a way as a self-defence mechanism, like a shell to protect the person from the outside world, which has become too painful.

Reduced personal accomplishment

Maslach and Jackson take "personal accomplishment" to mean notions of success and control over events. An individual suffering from burnout feels that they have no control over what happens to them: the situation is completely out of their hands. They feel unable to respond to the (unachievable) goals that they have often set for themselves. Eaten away at by a feeling of failure, frustration and discouragement, they feel that they are no good. Their self-image is at its lowest ebb.

Maslach and Jackson evaluate each of these three aspects through a series of questions. Taken together, these 22 questions make up what they call the Maslach Burnout Inventory (MBI). Their model has become established as a yardstick in the diagnosis of burnout.

A SLY AND INSIDIOUS ILLNESS

People do not succumb to burnout overnight. It is a slow, gradual process which takes the form of a cycle. The phenomenon can be divided into a number of phases, which are defined differently by different analysts.

Freudenberg and North's model (1985), which is considered as a reference model, comprises 12 stages. The phases do not necessarily follow the order outlined below: some may be skipped, others may take place simultaneously, etc. The length of each one varies between individuals.

1. The compulsion to prove oneself

You are bursting with energy and you give your work 100%. You only have one idea in your head: doing your best. You leave no room for mediocrity. You make it your mission to deliver quality at all costs. You are full of ambition and want to set an example. You are aiming for excellence and recognition.

2. Working harder

In your constant quest for perfection, you force yourself to stretch your limits. You do not think twice about working overtime or taking work home. Your moments of relaxation become rarer, as work takes up an increasingly large place in your mind.

3. Neglecting personal needs

More and more often, you find yourself sacrificing your hobbies and your free time for work. You go out less, cut meals short and give up your sleeping time. You are listening to your body less and less. You simply "don't have time for that".

4. Displacement of conflicts

You experience more and more periods of unease, stress and even panic. However, you are unable to identify the source of your worries. You tell yourself that "everything will turn out OK" and "it's just a rough patch". As tensions and conflicts emerge, you choose to run away from them.

5. Revision of values

Work has become your number one priority. Your traditional values fall by the wayside: you increasingly abandon your friends and family and isolate yourself. You also start to look at other people differently: you tolerate contradiction less and less, for example.

6. Denial of emerging problems

You are increasingly impatient and intolerant towards others. You may even become aggressive. According to you, if your worries are increasing, it is because of an overload of work, a lack of time or the incompetence of your colleagues.

7. Withdrawal

You do not go out any more and no longer feel the need (the desire?) to see other people. Your social interactions have been reduced to the bare minimum. The outside world has become too demanding, and there is a ball of anxiety that never leaves you. You may resort to substance abuse to get over the stress which is gnawing at you, for example by drinking or smoking more than usual.

8. Obvious behavioural changes

Fatigue, stress and loneliness have left their mark on you. Your loved ones say that they no longer recognise you: for example, you regularly hear that you have been "acting strangely" lately or that "something seems wrong". Essentially, you are the only one who has not noticed your change in attitude.

9. Depersonalisation

You feel that you have nothing good to offer any more. You have lost all confidence in yourself and your skills. Your self-esteem is at its lowest ebb. Your life is limited to a series of automatic actions, devoid of any emotion.

10. Inner emptiness

You feel a great sense of emptiness. You may desperately try to fill this emptiness through all kinds of excesses: tobacco, alcohol, drugs and sex, for example.

11. Depression

Exhausted, desperate and apathetic, you no longer take pleasure in anything: not in work, or in others, or in life. You feel downhearted, and the idea of a better future seems simply inconceivable to you.

12. Burnout syndrome

At this stage, you are at rock bottom. You can no longer see the light at the end of the tunnel, to the point where you are having suicidal thoughts. Your body and your mind are at the edge of collapse. You can see it now, but it is already well established: burnout has taken hold of you. Now, your only option is to get help urgently.

You have to agree that there is nothing tempting about this outline. Maybe you saw yourself in one of the descriptions, or maybe you saw one of your loved ones. In both cases, you have control over the situation: say no to this vicious circle before it's too late!

WHEN BURNOUT IS LYING IN WAIT

Although burnout is an insidious process, it is possible to identify the warning signs. Early detection of these symptoms allows you to slow down and halt the progression before you reach the point of no return. The following is an inexhaustive outline of analyses of the symptoms of burnout. In particular, it draws on studies by Freudenberger (1974), Cherniss (1980), Bährer-Kohler (2012) and Mone and London (2014). Generally speaking, the symptoms can be classified into three categories: psychological, behavioural and physical.

Psychological symptoms

The first psychological manifestation of burnout is, unsurprisingly, intense emotional fatigue. The individual suffering from burnout feels a constant sense of unease and stress. This anxiety, which sometimes verges on paranoia, causes the individual to become hypersensitive: they may lose their temper over the slightest thing, then burst into tears a minute later. This loss of control drives them into a corner, to the point of draining them of any emotion. Overwhelmed by a general feeling of failure and powerlessness, they can no longer fight against it. Discouragement has made them simply incapable of facing up to difficult situations, of concentrating, or even of listening. Eaten away at by guilt, they choose to isolate themselves and in this way wall themselves away in silence.

Behavioural symptoms

Unless you are very close to the person concerned, the psychological symptoms of burnout cannot be clearly detected. It is therefore in a colleague or an employee's day-to-day behaviour that you will spot the signs of burnout. More precisely, you will see burnout through changes in their behaviour. Previously highly committed and motivated, they now demonstrate a real aversion to work: when they turn up at all, they drag their feet and frequently check their watch. They are major procrastinators (they have a pathological tendency to put everything off), so they are unproductive and alarmingly slow and distracted. Their relationships with others have also completely changed: quiet and withdrawn, they avoid conversation and do not like to be contradicted. They are irritable and can behave impulsively or even aggressively. Their indifference and lack of empathy are combined with a worrying pessimism and cynicism.

Physical symptoms

Finally, burnout brings its share of physiological difficulties. These troubles are once again related to the inherent stress of the syndrome. The first symptom is of course intense, chronic physical fatigue. The person suffering from burnout regularly gets bad migraines and stomach aches. The tension can also cause muscle stiffness. They may have anxiety attacks, with an increased heart rate, high blood pressure and hyperventilation. Burnout can also cause physical symptoms specific to depression: sleep is disturbed (insomnia) and the individual loses their appetite and suffers from nausea or dizzy spells.

Whatever form they take, the symptoms of burnout closely resemble the symptoms of stress and depression, with the exception that their source is always found in the professional setting. By definition, a person suffering from burnout demonstrates an unfortunate tendency to not listen to their body. It is therefore up to those around them to pay attention to the warning signs and possible manifestations of the syndrome. If you suspect that someone close to you is affected by burnout, invite them to talk about it and to go see a specialist.

AN EXPLOSIVE COCKTAIL

You should now be able to identify the first signs of the vicious circle of burnout. But what factors lie at the root of the problem? Are some people at a higher risk than others? Are we all equal in the face of burnout? Dominique Rulkin, a work psychologist, explains that burnout is the result of a combination of factors, linked to three areas in particular: the professional context, the personal context and the interpersonal context.

The professional context

Burnout differs from stress and depression above all in the fact that its source can invariably be found in the work setting. In this area, multiple aspects come into play and risk leading the individual to snap.

The nature of the work itself can be a source of burnout. First of all, the task may demand a large amount of time and effort because of its complexity. The workload could also be particularly high. Furthermore, the work may involve a high degree of responsibility or have serious consequences, for other people for example. Finally, tight deadlines may be a factor which causes anxiety.

These specific demands of work as such are combined with other considerations which are specific to the professional environment and to office life. A negative atmosphere can in particular play a part in the development of the syndrome, as can being unable to find your place in the organisation and not sharing the spirit and values of the company. Poor general organisation (unclear instructions, material which is unsuitable for the requirements of the work, etc.) will also have a negative effect. Finally, we cannot forget one significant factor: a lack of recognition, which inevitably leads to low self-esteem.

The personal context

Although burnout is intrinsically linked to the professional environment, it is also exacerbated by some character traits that are inherent to the individual.

The most obvious of these is without a doubt the excessive commitment that an individual can show towards their work. The pressure the worker faces then is often qualitative: ambition and perfectionism push them to always do more. Exceptional commitment can also reflect an idealistic, not to mention utopian, nature.

Furthermore, people who tend to forget themselves in order to remain conscientious demonstrate a predisposition to burnout. The same goes for those with little self-confidence. A lack of assertiveness (the inability to say no) is another typical trait of candidates for burnout. People who struggle to delegate or to set limits will also find it difficult to establish a distinction between their professional and private lives. They are therefore at a higher risk of finding themselves in unmanageable situations.

Interpersonal context

All the individual's social relationships can also play a part in the development of the syndrome. Burnout is not a direct result of the state of a person's relationships with their friends, partner or family members. Nonetheless, difficulties in these areas can contribute to the stress that has already built up for a worker, hastening their collapse. Conversely, people who are well-supported and happy in their private lives will be less inclined to fall back on their work.

The coming together of these different risk factors, character traits and predispositions can result in an explosive cocktail. In general, you should always maintain a balance between your private life and professional life, and set limits from the beginning.

Ask yourself some key questions with regard to these three measurement scales:

- How do you view your work? Do you feel that you are in control of the situation? Do you feel intense fatigue?
- How would you define yourself on a personal level? Do you recognise yourself in the profile of at-risk individuals?
- How would you describe your social relationships? How do you view others?

TOP TIPS

- Don't do too much! Stick to reasonable working hours and avoid working lots of overtime or, even worse, bringing work home. When you feel that you need it, give yourself one or more days off. Remember than nobody is irreplaceable: the company won't fall apart without you.

SOMETHING TO AVOID

In the age of smartphones and hyperconnectivity, it is sometimes difficult to establish a clear distinction between work and private life. Nonetheless, learn to switch off, both in the literal and the figurative senses: in particular, avoid looking at your work emails outside work hours.

- Set yourself reasonable goals. It is good to have ambition, but it is even better to be able to distinguish between the possible and the impossible. The majority of candidates for burnout set themselves completely utopian goals, which only makes them more disillusioned. Challenge yourself, but respect your limits.
- Structure your work. Set priorities: what are the most important tasks? The most urgent? The most complex? Proceed step by step, referring to lists if you need to. This method allows you to understand your workload better.
- Learn to delegate. Avoid taking on an overly heavy workload by yourself: divide the tasks up. You will not

offend your colleagues if you give them work to do. On the contrary, you are showing that you have confidence in them.

- Keep listening to your needs. Give yourself half an hour to an hour for meals. Let yourself have a coffee break. Stick to a reasonable amount of sleep. Take time for breakfast (preferably as a family). Exercise.
- Believe in yourself. A major part of burnout is linked to self-esteem. The constant need for reassurance about your abilities leads to a (desperate) search for recognition, and therefore generally to doing too much. Take pride in what you are doing for your own sake.
- Put your professional relationships into perspective. A lack of human warmth can also play a role in the appearance of burnout. In addition, do not try to become friends with your colleagues at any cost, and do not take professional remarks too much to heart. Criticism is supposed to be constructive and is not a reflection on your personal qualities.
- Find support! Among the at-risk profiles, we find individuals who are less happy on a personal level and who tend to fall back on their work. Make the most of your weekends to meet the people you care about: appreciate family time, and plan outings with friends.

In a nutshell, make sure there is always a clear division between the professional setting and the private sphere. Don't let problems at the office encroach on the rest of your life. Keep in mind that work is a part of your life; it is not your whole life.

FAQS

HOW CAN BURNOUT BE RECOGNISED?

Burnout is a problem whose source can be found in the professional environment. This long, insidious process results mainly from the feelings of disillusionment, failure and despair which arise when a person has set themselves overly high expectations for their work.

Burnout refers to a general state of distress, and is characterised by intense fatigue which is felt on three levels in particular:

- emotional: the individual is exhausted and drained of their emotions;
- interpersonal: out of fear of suffering more, the individual isolates themselves from the outside world;
- personal: the individual is discouraged and loses all self-esteem.

As well as these three clear-cut warning signs, there are a whole host of psychological symptoms such as paranoia, behavioural symptoms such as procrastination, and physical symptoms such as migraines and stomach aches.

STRESS OR BURNOUT: WHEN SHOULD YOU WORRY?

The line between stress and burnout may seem unclear, as the two concepts are closely linked. Whereas stress can be caused by a multitude of factors of all kinds, burnout is always linked to the professional setting.

Furthermore, while people suffering from burnout constantly experience states of stress, the opposite is not always true. In other words, a stressed person will not necessarily be affected by burnout. In reality, everything depends on the individual's ability to manage their stress. When situations of stress become chronic and are accompanied by a loss of control over events, seeing a specialist is highly recommended.

ARE THERE ANY HIGH-RISK PROFESSIONS?

Although anybody can experience burnout, we can nonetheless note that some professions present more cases of burnout than others. Among the most affected sectors are the following:

- the "helping" professions, such as healthcare (doctors and medical staff), social work, etc.;
- education: teachers, trainers, educators, etc.;
- professions linked to safety, for example the fire brigade, the police, civil protection, etc.

Generally speaking, jobs where relationships with others play a major role seem to be more exposed to burnout.

IS BURNOUT AN ILLNESS?

Burnout is not an illness in the clinical sense of the term. It is defined as a syndrome which, to take the definition of the

Collins English Dictionary, is "a symptom, characteristic, or set of symptoms or characteristics indicating the existence of a condition, problem, etc".

In addition, burnout cannot be considered as a personality disorder in the same way as, for example, neurosis or schizophrenia. It is a change in behaviour following a long, continuous period of stress.

IS BURNOUT RECOGNISED BY THE LAW?

Some countries are starting to officially recognise burnout: for example, legislation which came into effect in Belgium on 1 September 2014 means that a Committee for Prevention and Protection at Work must carry out a risk analysis and take the necessary measures to counter "psychosocial risks" within the company. Furthermore, an employee suffering from burnout can submit a request for intervention via an internal procedure.

Although burnout is not currently classified as a work-related illness in the UK, there is increasing recognition of the condition, and legislation to protect workers and minimise their risk of burnout remains a possibility for the future.

IS BURNOUT CONTAGIOUS?

Given that the primary cause of burnout is the professional environment, it is not rare for several workers in the same company, or even the same department, to all be affected by the syndrome. The reason for this phenomenon could be, for example, organisational measures: employees affected by reorganisation are less motivated and complain more. Thus, the negative working environment fuels the risk of burnout.

From there, it does not require a big leap to conclude that burnout is contagious. This is why it is important to have a prevention and protection committee at work to stave off the development of the syndrome in the company.

WHO SHOULD YOU TALK TO IF YOU ARE EXPERIENCING BURNOUT?

From the first warning signs of burnout, it is good to ask an expert for advice. The person best able to help you is your usual doctor, as they know you and can therefore easily identify any changes in your behaviour.

You can also talk to the prevention adviser in your company, if there is one, or to a professional coach. Unlike a doctor, who will tend to focus on medical treatment to alleviate your various symptoms, a coach will support you through your recovery process by giving you the tools to better manage your stress on a daily basis.

In the most severe cases of burnout, psychotherapy and/or psychiatric treatment are possibilities.

OVER TO YOU

24 years after Maslach and Jackson's model, Kristensen (2005) put forward a test designed to anticipate and diagnose burnout. The Copenhagen Burnout Inventory (CBI) comprises 19 questions, divided between the three axes of burnout: personal, work-based and client-based.

Below you will find the questions which make up the CBI. You can take the test in order to evaluate your level of burnout. Although the result does not constitute a valid medical diagnosis, it does allow you to judge whether it might be worth seeing a doctor.

Complete each statement and add up the total number of points. "Clients" should be taken to mean the people you are in contact with as part of your work.

Personal burnout

	PERSONAL BURNOUT	Never/ almost never	Seldom	Some-times	Often	Always
		To a very low degree	To a low degree	Some-what	To a high degree	To a very high degree
1	How often do you feel tired?	0	1	2	3	4
2	How often are you physically exhausted?	0	1	2	3	4
3	How often are you emotionally exhausted?	0	1	2	3	4
4	How often do you think: "I can't take it anymore"?	0	1	2	3	4
5	How often do you feel worn out?	0	1	2	3	4
6	How often do you feel weak and susceptible to illness?	0	1	2	3	4

Results

- < 13: you show few or no signs of personal burnout.
- 13-17: you show some signs of personal burnout; something to keep an eye on.

- > 17: your work is causing you physical and psychological burnout.

Work-related burnout

WORK-RELATED BURNOUT		Never/ almost never	Seldom	Some-times	Often	Always
		To a very low degree	To a low degree	Some-what	To a high degree	To a very high degree
7	Do you feel worn out at the end of the working day?	0	1	2	3	4
8	Are you exhausted in the morning at the thought of another day at work?	0	1	2	3	4
9	Do you feel that every working hour is tiring for you?	0	1	2	3	4
10	Do you have enough energy for friends and family during leisure time?	0	1	2	3	4
11	Is your work emotionally exhausting?	0	1	2	3	4
12	Does your work frustrate you?	0	1	2	3	4
13	Do you feel burnt out because of your work?	0	1	2	3	4

Results

- < 15: you show few or no signs of work-related burnout.
- 15-19: you show some signs of work-related burnout; something to keep an eye on.
- > 19: your work is causing you physical and psychological burnout.

Client-related burnout

CLIENT-RELATED BURNOUT		Never/ almost never	Seldom	Some-times	Often	Always
		To a very low degree	To a low degree	Some-what	To a high degree	To a very high degree
14	Do you find it hard to work with clients?	0	1	2	3	4
15	Does it drain your energy to work with clients?	0	1	2	3	4
16	Do you find it frustrating to work with clients?	0	1	2	3	4
17	Do you feel that you give more than you get back when you work with clients?	0	1	2	3	4
18	Are you tired of working with clients?	0	1	2	3	4
19	Do you some-times wonder how long you will be able to continue working with clients?	0	1	2	3	4

Results

- < 13: you show few or no signs of client-related burnout.
- 13-17: you show some signs of client-related burnout; something to keep an eye on.
- > 17: your work is causing you physical and psychological burnout.

We want to hear from you!
Leave a comment on your online library
and share your favourite books on social media!

FURTHER READING

BIBLIOGRAPHY

- Association France Burn Out (2015) *Reconnaissance de la maladie professionnelle.* [Online]. [Accessed 4 November 2016]. Available from: <http://asso-franceburnout.fr/reconnaissance-de-la-maladie-professionnelle/>
- Bährer-Kohler, S. (2012) *Burnout for Experts: Prevention in the Context of Living and Working.* New York: Springer Science and Business Media.
- Bradley, H. (1969) Community-Based Treatment for Young Adult Offenders. *Crime and Delinquency.* 15(3), pp. 359-370.
- Cherniss, C. (1980) *Staff Burnout: Job Stress in the Human Services.* California: SAGE Publications.
- Cogen, P. (2015) Burnout. Questionnaire CBI (Copenhagen Burnout Inventory). *Thérapie Brève.* [Online]. [Accessed 4 November 2016]. Available from: <https://www.therapiebreve.be/plus/tests/burnout-cbi>
- Freudenberger, H. (1987) Staff burn-out. *Journal of Social Issues.* 30(1), pp. 159-165.
- Freudenberger, H. (1987) *L'Épuisement Professionnel: La Brûlure Interne.* Chicoutimi (Quebec): Gäetan Morin.
- Freudenberger, H. and North, G. (1985) *Women's Burnout. How to Spot It, How to Reverse It and How to Prevent It.* New York: Doubleday.
- Kristensen, T., Borritz, M., Villadsen, E., and Christensen, K. (2005) The Copenhagen Burnout Inventory: a new tool for the assessment of burnout. *Work and Stress.* 19(3), pp. 192-207.

- Maslach, C. (1976) Burned-out. *Human Behaviour.* 9(5), pp. 16-22.
- Maslach, C. and Jackson, S. (1981) The measurement of experienced burnout. *Journal of Occupational Behaviour.* 2(2), pp. 99-113.
- Mone, E. and London, M. (2014) *Employee Engagement Through Effective Performance Management: A Practical Guide for Managers.* New York: Routledge.
- Munster, J.-F. (2014) Le burn-out reconnu par la loi dès le 1er septembre. *Le Soir.* [Online]. [Accessed 4 November 2016]. Available from: <http://www.lesoir.be/638235/article/actualite/sciences-et-sante/2014-08-28/burn-out-reconnu-par-loi-des-1er-septembre>
- Rulkin, D. (No date) Dossier burn-out. *Le Psychologue.* [Online]. [Accessed 4 November 2016]. Available from: <https://www.lepsychologue.be/articles/burn-out-sommaire.php?PHPSESSID=b3f07898bbd4cce5518e46a6d3ea5067>

ADDITIONAL SOURCES

- Bourg Carter, S. (2013) The tell tale signs of burnout...do you have them? *Psychology Today.* [Online]. [Accessed 4 November 2016]. Available from: <https://www.psychologytoday.com/blog/high-octane-women/201311/the-tell-tale-signs-burnout-do-you-have-them>
- Freudenberger, H. and Richelson, G. (1985) *Burnout: The High Cost of High Achievement.* London: Arrow Books Ltd.
- The Guardian (2016) *Stressed and exhausted: spot the signs of burnout before it hits you.* [Online]. [Accessed

4 November 2016]. Available from: <https://www.
theguardian.com/women-in-leadership/2016/jan/21/
spot-the-signs-of-burnout-before-it-hits-you>

- Maslach, C. and Leiter, M. P. (2008) Early predictors
  of job burnout and engagement. *Journal of Applied
  Psychology*. Volume 93, pp. 498–512.
- Shaufeli, W. B., Leiter, M. P. and Maslach, C. (2009)
  Burnout: Thirty-five years of research and practice.
  Career Development International. 14, pp. 204–220.

IMPROVE YOUR GENERAL KNOWLEDGE

IN A BLINK OF AN EYE !

www.50minutes.com

www.50minutes.com

Ebook EAN: 9782806269782

Paperback EAN: 9782806291233

Legal Deposit: D/2016/12603/866

Cover: © Primento

Digital conception by Primento, the digital partner of publishers.